INTRODUCTION

Hey! I'm Cali Black, and I'm *kind of obsessed* with scripture study.

People ask me all the time what my favorite scripture study tips are, and even though I could talk your ear off for hours with the ideas that I have, my strategies always boil down to 2 main points:

1. Figure out the context of a scripture story before you start reading so that your brain has a fighting chance at comprehension.

2. Ask yourself questions after every single section that you read in order to apply the teachings and change your behavior.

When I do these 2 things before and during my daily scripture study, the personal revelation flows. I ponder instead of speed-reading. I grow a little better every day.

So when I looked at other study guides out there, I realized that there weren't any that did everything that I wanted them to! There are amazing study guides that give you all the historical background and interesting facts. And there are other study guides that just focus on the spiritual takeaways from certain verses.

I thought: Why not make the kind of study guide that I'm actually looking for? One that covers both the context (BIG picture) and those spiritual application questions (LITTLE picture)?

And so, I did. I created a whole batch of these Big Picture/Little Picture Study Guides for the Book of Mormon, and put them out there into the world to see if anyone else would like this kind of study guide, too. It turned out that this type of simple fusion between background information AND spiritual lessons was in high demand.

I know that the thought of studying the Doctrine and Covenants can strike fear into hearts. So I understood that I needed to create a Big Picture/Little Picture Study Guide that would hit just the right balance of background info and spiritual questions for this book of scripture.

And here it is.

Thank you for all your support. I know that as you use this study guide in tangent with your Come, Follow Me manual and the Doctrine and Covenants, you CAN understand these stories, and they CAN change your life.

Happy Studying!

Cali Black

@ComeFollowMeStudy
ComeFollowMeStudy.com

DIRECTIONS

How to use this Big Picture/Little Picture Study Guide

big picture

Think of this part as the super-simple glossary that gives you a glimpse into history. You'll learn exactly what you need to know to feel like you are really "understanding" the stories, but not so much info that you feel like you've just been handed a textbook.

The Big Picture section is not meant to be read all the way through in one sitting (although if you want to, go for it!).

Instead, when you sit down to study, glance through the entries for the people or places that the section covers.

And to make it super easy, I've also **BOLDED** the sections in each person's description! So if you are studying a Section with Oliver Cowdery in it, but you don't want to read through his whole entry, just scan the words 'til you see the Section number bolded like this: **[Section 8]**. Read some of my bullet points around the Section number that you are studying, and you'll be totally caught up on the context!

little picture

This is my favorite part - where I help you totally focus in on the single Section that you are studying!

Each page has its own Section in the Doctrine and Covenants, so turn to the page of the Section you are studying when you sit down each day.

You'll see "at-a-glance" facts at the top of the page so that you can be reminded:

- Who this revelation was THROUGH (hint: they're all through Joseph Smith! But I just wanted you to be aware that ALL of these revelations in Sections 1-70 came via the Lord through Joseph)
- Who this revelation was TO (sometimes it's one person, sometimes it was to the whole church...)
- Where and when the revelation occurred (this can help if you want to look up the location in the Big Picture portion!)

You'll learn what makes this Section unique, and get a short summary of what the contents are.

And then here's where the rubber meets the road: I give you THREE questions for every single Section in the Doctrine and Covenants that will help you apply what you just read to your personal life. If you've struggled applying scriptures in the past, this is going to transform your study! You are welcome to write down your answers, or they can serve as discussion questions with friends or family. I do recommend that you try to answer them in any way that you can though - this is what will change you!

I hope that you enjoy your study of the Doctrine and Covenants this year, and that this resource becomes an invaluable guide as you explore church history. Now, let's go!

DOCTRINE & COVENANTS

Part 1, Sections 1-70

big picture

*Keep track of the important people and places to
know with this quick, bullet-point reference guide.*

come
follow me
study
WITH CALI BLACK

PEOPLE

(In alphabetical order by last name)

Wheeler Baldwin

- Wheeler lived in Ohio, and was converted and baptized by Solomon Hancock in early 1831. In June, Wheeler was called to travel to Missouri and preach the gospel on the way there along with his companion, William Carter **[Section 52]**.

Heman Bassett

- Heman had lived on the Isaac Morley farm in Kirtland, Ohio, and was converted with most of his congregation when Oliver and the other brethren came to preach. In June of 1831, Heman had his blessings removed due to transgression at a church conference **[Section 52]**.

Titus Billings

- Titus was Isaac Morely's brother-in-law, and the second person baptized in Kirtland after Oliver and the other brethren came through.
- In August of 1831, Titus was asked to get rid of the farm so that he could journey to Missouri in the spring **[Section 63]**.

Ezra Booth

- Ezra joined the church after seeing Joseph heal a paralyzed woman's arm. He later traveled with the prophet and his companion Isaac Morley from Kirtland to Missouri for the first look at where Zion would be built **[Section 52]**. Ezra was not impressed, and quarreled with Joseph on the way back to Kirtland.
- The Lord mentioned that he had not kept the laws or commandments during a revelation in September 1831 **[Section 64]**, and Ezra published a letter in the local newspaper accusing Joseph of hiding secret plans from the public and making false prophecies. This actually ended up prompting Joseph to publish his revelations thus far in the "Book of Commandments", the precursor to the Doctrine and Covenants.

Reynolds Cahoon

- Reynolds lived in Kirtland, Ohio, where he heard the gospel and was baptized. In June of 1831, he was called at a church conference to travel to Missouri and preach the gospel on the way there, along with his companion Samuel Smith **[Section 52]**.

Jared Carter

- Jared learned about the Book of Mormon while traveling for business in New York, and within a few months, moved his family to join the church in Ohio.
- He was ordained a priest at a church conference in June of 1831 **[Section 52]** and served many missions immediately following his conversion.

Simeon Carter

- Simeon was baptized in Ohio in early 1831. In June, he was called at a church conference to travel to Missouri and preach the gospel on the way there, along with his companion Solomon Hancock **[Section 52]**.

William Carter

- William was called at a church conference in June of 1831 to travel to Missouri and preach the gospel on the way there along with his companion, Wheeler Baldwin **[Section 52]**.

Joseph Coe

- Joseph Coe was converted in New York, and made the transition to Ohio with the saints.
- In June of 1831, he was asked to be among the few moving to Missouri **[Section 55]**.

Zebedee Coltrin

- Zebedee was baptized into the church in Ohio. In June of 1831, he was called to travel to Missouri with his companion Levi Hancock, and preach the gospel on the way there **[Section 52]**.

Leman Copley

- Leman was a previous member of Sidney Rigdon's congregation who became converted to the gospel. He offered the saints coming from Colesville, New York a place to stay at his farm in Thompson, Ohio.
- He had previously followed some of the Shaker beliefs and interacted with the nearby Shaker community. In May 1831, Leman spoke with Joseph, and Joseph received a revelation refuting elements of the Shaker religion. Leman went with Sidney and Parley to the Shaker community and shared this document, but it was not received well **[Section 49]**.
- In June 1831, following the Shaker incident, Leman suddenly evicted all of the saints living on his farm and refused to house any of them, causing big issues for Newel Knight, their leader, and Edward Partridge, the local bishop **[Section 54]**.

John Corrill

- John was baptized in Ohio, and shortly thereafter was called to serve a short mission in a nearby county. In May of 1831, Joseph gave him a revelation that John was called to labor in the vineyard **[Section 50]**.
- In June, he was called to travel to Missouri and preach the gospel with Lyman Wight as his companion **[Section 52]**.

James Covel

- James was a respected Methodist minister who attended a church conference in January 1831, lingering afterward for 3 days. Joseph received a revelation for James where he was asked to be baptized and then travel to Ohio with the rest of the church **[Section 39]**.
- After just 2 days, James rejected the counsel due to his desires to stay on the east coast, and Joseph received another revelation for him **[Section 40]** before he returned home.

Oliver Cowdery

- Oliver Cowdery was a young school teacher who lived at the Smith family home in Manchester, after Joseph and Emma had already moved out to Harmony. Oliver learned about Joseph's visions and golden plates, and naturally became very curious. He told his good friend David Whitmer that he was going to try and figure out whether Joseph was telling the truth.
- Oliver received a private and serious spiritual revelation that helped him know that he should become Joseph's new scribe. After the school year was done, he went with Samuel Smith to Harmony, Pennsylvania, and stopped by David Whitmer's family home to tell him he was going to meet Joseph.
- Oliver showed up in Pennsylvania to help Joseph translate in April 1829, and was given a revelation about inquiring in faith **[Section 6]**. Oliver began as Joseph's scribe!
- That same month, Oliver and Joseph received revelations about John the Beloved **[Section 7]**, Oliver's desire to translate the plates **[Section 8]**, and the Lord's command to Oliver to have patience with his current assignment as scribe **[Section 9]**.
- After pondering about baptism, as was translated in the Book of Mormon, Oliver and Joseph received the Aaronic priesthood from John the Baptist on May 15, 1829 near Harmony **[Section 13]**. Joseph and Oliver baptized each other.
- Oliver reached out to his friend David Whitmer, and asked if David's parents, Peter and Mary, would host Joseph, Emma, and Oliver as they finished the translation, due to growing oppression in Harmony, Pennsylvania. They agreed, and the three of them moved to the Whitmer home in Fayette, New York.
- After the completion of the translation in the Whitmer home, Oliver, David, and Martin Harris had a desire to become one of the Three Witnesses to the gold plates. Oliver was called to be one of the Three Witnesses in June 1829 **[Section 17]** and saw an angel, along with the plates and other relics.

- Oliver played a huge role in officially organizing the church. He asked Joseph questions about it as early as June 1829, and received a revelation calling him to repentance **[Section 18]**. The church was officially organized April 6, 1830, and Oliver and Joseph were ordained as the presiding officers and elders of the church **[Section 21]**. His duties were also further clarified in another revelation **[Section 23]**.
- Around this time, Oliver was a scribe for a short period of time for Joseph's translation of the Bible **[Section 35]**.
- Oliver received more revelations, along with Joseph, in July of 1830 **[Sections 24, 26]**. In September of that year, he was asked to correct Hiram's false revelations, and officially called to serve a mission to the Native American tribes in Western Missouri **[Section 28]**.
- Parley, Peter Jr., and Ziba Peterson were also called to accompany Oliver on his mission, and they all went to Kirtland. In Kirtland, they converted many, and Frederick G. Williams joined them as they traveled to western Missouri and taught some Native American tribes. Oliver was later released from his calling as church historian, being replaced by John Whitmer **[Section 47]**.
- In the summer of 1831, Oliver and William W. Phelps were asked to work together in printing and editing books in Missouri **[Sections 55 and 57]**. Shortly afterwards, Oliver was told that he should return to Ohio with Joseph and Sidney **[Sections 58, 60, and 61]**.
- In November 1831, when Joseph and the brethren decided to publish Joseph's revelations in the "Book of Commandments", Oliver tried writing a preface to the book, but quickly learned that the Lord's revelations were better. Oliver was asked to spread the teachings about raising righteous children to the saints in Zion **[Section 68]**.
- Oliver and John Whitmer were tasked with taking the manuscripts for the new Book of Commandments from Hiram, Ohio to Missouri **[Section 69]**, and Oliver was reminded that he should be a good steward for the church **[Section 70]**.

Edson Fuller

- Edson lived in Ohio, where he was converted and baptized. At a church conference in June of 1831, he was called to travel to Missouri with Jacob Scott and preach the gospel on the way there, although it seems like he never actually went **[Section 52]**.

Algernon Sidney Gilbert (Sidney Gilbert)

- Sidney was a storekeeper along with Newel K. Whitney in Kirtland.
- After Sidney's conversion, he requested to know his calling, and was given a revelation to forsake the world and endure to the end in June of 1831 **[Section 53]**.
- Sidney moved to Independence, Missouri, and was asked to start a store in July of 1831 **[Section 57]**. He was encouraged to work quickly in his errand and mission **[Section 61]**.
- Sidney returned to Ohio for some time, but in September, the Lord told him to make plans to return to his store in Missouri soon. However, even though he was returning to Missouri, Sidney was told to not sell all of his possessions in Ohio **[Section 64]**.

Selah J. Griffin

- Selah was a resident in Kirtland, who was converted and baptized when the saints moved into town. In June 1831, he was called to travel to Missouri and preach the gospel on the way there **[Section 52]**. Selah was originally assigned to travel with Newel Knight as his companion, but after Newel realized he needed to help the saints in Thompson, Ohio figure out their living situation, and Ezra Thayre's call was revoked due to unrighteousness, Selah was ultimately assigned to travel with Thomas B. Marsh (Ezra's assigned companion) **[Section 56]**.

Levi W. Hancock

- Levi was converted to the gospel in Ohio as a result of Oliver, Parley, Peter Jr. and Ziba's preaching on their way to the Native Americans. He became concerned with how some people acted when "filled with the spirit" once the 4 men left, and was relieved when Joseph moved to Ohio, rebuking evil spirits and discerning between light and darkness.
- In June of 1831, he was called to travel to Missouri and preach the gospel on the way there, along with his companion Zebedee Coltrin **[Section 52]**.

Solomon Hancock

- Solomon was baptized in November of 1830 in Ohio. In June of 1831, he was called to travel to Missouri along with his companion Simeon Carter, and preach the gospel on the way there. **[Section 52]**.

Martin Harris

- Martin was older and wealthier than Joseph. They became good friends while Joseph was waiting for the gold plates.
- When Joseph needed to move to Harmony, Pennsylvania with his wife to escape the persecution and those trying to steal the plates, Martin gave him $50 as a gift to help get him there.
- Martin took a copy of some of the characters to scholars in New York, and got confirmation that the characters were a reformed Egyptian, before scholars learned where the characters came from.
- Martin followed Joseph to Harmony, and took over for Emma as Joseph's scribe. Martin's wife, Lucy, also stayed with them for a bit, but was skeptical that Joseph never showed anyone the plates.
- Martin wanted to show his wife some of the transcriptions so that she would be pleased that he was investing money in the church, and asked Joseph for some of the manuscript pages. After being given some, he lost them, and felt great remorse when he had to tell Joseph.
- After hanging out in Palmyra for a while, he went and visited Joseph in Harmony to see how he was doing. He was delighted that Joseph had been forgiven of the Lord and was preparing to start translating again. Joseph received a revelation in March 1829 **[Section 5]** that tells Martin to believe Joseph's testimony, and that Martin can be a witness to the Book of Mormon at some point.
- A few months later, and with a strong desire to be one of the Three Witnesses, he was called to be one, along with Oliver Cowdery and David Whitmer **[Section 17]**. Although Martin originally felt he wasn't worthy to see the plates, he was a witness in June 1829.

- Joseph was ready to publish the Book of Mormon, although he would need a lot of money for any publisher to agree. **[Section 19]** Joseph Smith received a revelation where the Lord called Martin to repentance, and asked him to finance the printing of the Book of Mormon, and pay off other debts. In the summer of 1829, Martin did this, and the Book of Mormon was printed!
- After the transition to Ohio, he was called to travel to Missouri with his companion Edward Partridge on a short mission in June of 1831 **[Section 52]**. While in Missouri, he was asked to give money to the Bishop, and repent **[Section 58]**.
- Back in Ohio in November 1831, Martin was told to be a good steward of the church **[Section 70]**.

Solomon Humphrey

- Solomon was baptized into the church in the fall of 1830 in western New York. He followed the church's move to Kirland, Ohio, and in June 1831, he was called to travel to the eastern states and preach the gospel on the way there with Joseph Wakefield as his companion **[Section 52]**.

Orson Hyde

- Orson was a resident of Kirtland who, after much protest, was converted and baptized in October 1831.
- He was called to teach the gospel and to be of good cheer in November **[Section 68]**.

George James

- Following his conversion, he was ordained a priest at a church conference in Ohio in June of 1831 **[Section 52]**.

Luke S. Johnson

- Luke was the son of John Johnson, the home in Hiram, Ohio where Joseph and Emma lived for a while.
- He was called to teach the gospel and to be of good cheer in November of 1831 **[Section 68]**.

Lyman E. Johnson

- Lyman was the son of John Johnson, the home in Hiram, Ohio where Joseph and Emma lived for a while.
- He was called to teach the gospel and to be of good cheer in November of 1831 **[Section 68]**.

Joseph Knight, Sr

- Joseph Knight Sr. hired Joseph Smith to work on his farm, and ultimately became a great friend to the Smith family. He was even present when Joseph finally arrived home after obtaining the gold plates. The Knight family lived in Colesville, New York.
- Joseph Knight sent some supplies and money to Joseph and Emma while they were translating the plates in Harmony. Joseph received a revelation for Joseph Knight in May 1829 **[Section 12]**.
- After the Book of Mormon had been published and the church had been organized, Joseph Knight asked Joseph what his duties should be in the new church, along with 4 other brethren. In April 1830, Joseph Smith received a revelation that Joseph Knight needed to pray vocally and in secret, and that he should be baptized while using his words to preach **[Section 23]**. Joseph and his wife, Polly, were later baptized and confirmed members of the church, despite great opposition in Colesville where they resided.
- After Joseph Smith's revelation to move the saints to Ohio, Joseph Knight, his family, and his community of saints in Colesville traveled to Thompson, Ohio, where they resided for a while. Eventually, they were the first community to move to Missouri and started Zion. Unfortunately, his wife, Polly Knight, was the first saint to die in Zion, Jackson County in August of 1831 **[Section 59]**.

Newel Knight

- Newel was the son of Joseph Knight Sr., and his family were dear friends to Joseph, Emma, and the Smiths. They resided in Colesville, New York, in one of the most tight-knit groups of newly converted saints. After the Knight family was baptized, Hyrum Smith was their local leader for a while, until Newel Knight became the leader.
- Newel helped all of the saints in Colesville make the transition to Ohio, settling in Thompson, Ohio.
- Newel was initially called to serve a mission in Missouri in June of 1831 **[Section 52]**, but was told that he could stay with his congregation of saints in Thompson (formerly from Colesville) in order to help them out with some issues with the Law of Consecration and their land owner Leman Copley.
- Newel learned through a revelation from Joseph that his entire community was to move to Missouri in June 1831, thus making them the first migration of an entire branch of saints to Missouri **[Sections 54 and 56]**.

Thomas B. Marsh

- Thomas was a former printer's apprentice who traveled from Boston to western New York, searching for spiritual guidance and a new church. He eventually found Joseph and was given 16 pages of the manuscript of the Book of Mormon that was in the final preparation stages for printing. Thomas and his wife Elizabeth were both converted from these pages.
- After being baptized and ordained an elder, and after a church conference in September 1830, Thomas received a revelation through Joseph Smith where he was called to preach the word, and promised success and safety to his family **[Section 31]**.
- In June 1831, Thomas was called to travel to Missouri and preach the gospel on the way there, along with his companion Ezra Thayre **[Section 52]**. However, Ezra's call was later revoked due to unrighteousness, so Thomas was assigned to go with Selah J. Griffin **[Section 56]**.

William E. McLellin

- After losing his new wife and baby, William heard David Whitmer preaching and became converted. He followed David to Independence, Missouri, where Hyrum baptized him. He then traveled down to Kirtland to find Joseph.
- William had asked the Lord five specific questions in prayer, and then asked Joseph for a revelation without revealing the questions he had asked. In October 1831, Joseph received a revelation answering all of William's questions, including calling him on a mission to the eastern states **[Section 66]**. The following month, he was told to teach the gospel and be of good cheer **[Section 68]**.
- When Joseph and the elders of the church decided to publish Joseph's revelations in the "Book of Commandments" in November of 1831, William tried to write a preface and rewrite a revelation using elevated language, but failed.

Isaac Morley

- He lived in Kirtland and was a member of Sidney Rigdon's congregation prior to their conversion. He owned a farm where many members of Sidney's congregation lived communally. Many of them were converted when Parley, Oliver, John, and Ziba came into town in late 1830.
- In June of 1831, Isaac was called to travel to Missouri with his companion Ezra Booth and preach the gospel on the way there **[Section 52]**.
- After Isaac's return to Ohio, Joseph received a revelation telling Isaac that he had broken the commandments, but had been forgiven. He was given a tender reminder that he would not be tempted above that which he can bear **[Section 64]**.

John Murdock

- John was baptized in November 1830 in Kirtland, and started preaching the gospel immediately. It was his wife who passed away during childbirth to twins, and he gave the twins to Emma and Joseph.
- In June of 1831, he was called to travel to Missouri for a mission and preach the gospel along the way **[Section 52]**. Hyrum Smith was assigned as his companion.

Hiram Page

- He was married to Catherine Whitmer (David Whitmer's sister, and Peter and Mary's daughter). In June of 1829, he was able to be one of the Eight Witnesses to the Book of Mormon on the Smith farm in Manchester.
- In September 1830, after the organization of the church, Hiram had a stone where he was claiming to receive revelation for the entire church. A concerned Joseph received a revelation asking Oliver to speak with Hiram and correct his errors of deception **[Section 28]**.

Edward Partridge

- Edward was a member of Sidney Rigdon's congregation in Kirtland, and following Sidney's conversion, Edward and Sidney traveled to New York in order to meet Joseph. Edward was given a revelation from Joseph in December 1830 that Sidney would give him the Holy Spirit **[Section 36]**.
- After the big move back to Kirtland, Edward was called as the first Bishop because of his pure heart in February 1831 **[Section 41]**. He was even asked to continue serving as Bishop in Kirtland, even though others were being called to serve missions **[Section 42]**.
- Edward helped the saints arriving from New York become established, and Joseph gave him a few revelations in May 1831 **[Sections 50-51]**. Edward was then called to travel to Missouri with his companion Martin Harris and other brethren in what he assumed would be a short mission, beginning in June 1831 **[Section 52]**. However, once in Missouri, he was given a revelation that he needed to stay there in order to help the saints divide the land as they arrived **[Section 57]**.
- In August and September of 1831, Edward received revelations where the Lord asked him to repent, and gave him assignments to continue working **[Section 58 and 64]**. He tirelessly worked to help the saints arriving in Independence, Missouri provisions and get them settled on land.

Ziba Peterson

- Ziba became converted and joined the church in Fayette. He felt a desire to teach the Native Americans, so Joseph gave Ziba and Parley a revelation that they could go join Oliver and Peter on their mission in October of 1830 **[Section 32]**. Ziba traveled through Kirtland and to Missouri along with the rest of the men.

William W. Phelps

- William W. Phelps had been converted in New York soon after the church's organization, but he was not baptized until he arrived in Kirtland with his family in June of 1831. Joseph received a revelation telling him to print and write books for children for the church schools, and asking him to move to Missouri **[Section 55]**.
- Once in Missouri, William was asked to set up a printing shop **[Section 57]**.
- William was also warned to stay meek and work quickly on his errands **[Sections 57 and 58]**.
- In November of 1831, William's printing press was tasked with publishing the Book of Commandments. Initially, the plan was to print 10,000 copies, but it later got changed to 3,000 copies **[Section 67]**. He was also reminded to be a good steward with the things he had been blessed with **[Section 70]**.

Orson Pratt

- Orson was Parley P. Pratt's younger brother.
- Orson was just 19 years old when he was converted by his older brother, and received a revelation from Joseph in November of 1830 **[Section 34]**. Orson served a short mission to the people in Colesville, New York.
- He traveled to Ohio with the rest of the saints, and during a church conference in June of 1831, he was called to travel to Missouri with his brother Parley and preach the gospel on the way there **[Section 52]**.

Parley P. Pratt

- Parley was a farmer who felt the Spirit nudging him to sell his farm and preach of spiritual gifts. Eventually, he was given a Book of Mormon, traveled to Palmyra, and met Hyrum. Hyrum taught Parley quite a bit, and then invited him to come to the Whitmer farm in Fayette to meet more church members. Parley was baptized.
- Sometime in October 1830, Parley converted his younger brother, Orson Pratt **[Section 34]**.
- Shortly after his baptism, Parley was called by the Lord to join Oliver on his mission to the West in October 1830 **[Section 32]**. Peter Jr. and Ziba Peterson were to join the mission, too. On their way to Missouri, Parley stopped by Kirtland, Ohio to talk to his former pastor, Sidney Rigdon.
- While in Kirtland, Parley gave Sidney a Book of Mormon, and Sidney was converted, thus converting many of his congregation members, too.
- After spending time in Kirtland, the group of missionaries headed to western Missouri and preached to the Native Americans.
- Later, back in Ohio, Parley was given a revelation (along with Sidney and Leman) refuting elements of the Shaker religion. In May 1831, the local Shaker community did not accept the refutations **[Section 49]**.
- Sidney was asked to strengthen the church around him **[Section 50]**, and then to travel to Missouri with Joseph, his brother Orson, and other brethren in June of 1831 **[Section 52]**.

Sidney Rigdon

- Sidney Rigdon was a preacher who lived in Kirtland, Ohio. He had previously been Parley P. Pratt's pastor, so when Parley and others came through Kirtland on their way to their mission to the Native Americans, Parley stopped by to see Sidney and urge him to join the church.
- Sidney was quickly converted, and immediately, many in his congregation were converted as well, almost doubling the size of the small church membership at the time.
- Sidney took his friend Edward Partridge and traveled to New York in December 1830 to meet Joseph. Sidney was given a revelation that greater things were awaiting him, and telling him that he should be Joseph's new scribe for the Bible translation **[Section 35]**.
- Later that month, Sidney was with Joseph when he received the revelation to stop translating and move the church to Ohio **[Section 37]**. He was also present when Joseph received revelation about James Covel's rejection **[Section 40]**.
- Sidney moved back to Ohio at the same time as Joseph, and the Bible translation started back up again in February 1831 **[Section 41]**. Sidney was present when "the Law" was given in a conference, and when Joseph received word that the church should plan a conference [Sections 42 and 44]. Sidney later learned that the conference would be in Missouri, and that he would travel there with Joseph and others **[Section 52]**.
- In May 1831, Sidney received a revelation (along with Parley and Leman) that refuted elements of the Shaker religion. The local Shaker community did not accept this **[Section 49]**.
- Once Sidney had arrived in Missouri in August 1831, he was asked to write an epistle and description of the land, and to consecrate and dedicate the land for the future temple in Missouri. Sidney was then told to return back to Ohio along with Joseph and others, although he was told not to preach until arriving in Cincinnati **[Sections 58, 60, and 61]**. However, the Lord told Sidney that he was not pleased with his writing efforts, because he was exalting himself in his own heart **[Section 63]**.
- In November 1831, when Joseph and the brethren decided to publish Joseph's revelations in the "Book of Commandments", Sidney tried writing a preface to the book, but quickly learned that the Lord's revelations were much better. Sidney was also reminded that he should be a good steward of the church **[Section 70]**.

Simonds Ryder

- Simonds had resided in Hiram, Ohio before the saints arrived, and was converted shortly thereafter. He was given blessings at a church conference in June of 1831 **[Section 52]**.

Jacob Scott

- In Ohio, Jacob was called at a church conference to travel to Missouri and preach the gospel on the way there, along with his companion Edson Fuller **[Section 52]**.

Emma Hale Smith

- Emma met Joseph when he was hired to work near her family farm in Harmony, Pennsylvania. Her parents did not like Joseph, but Emma and Joseph eventually got married and moved in with his parents in Manchester, New York in January of 1827.
- Emma was the first scribe for Joseph's translation of the Book of Mormon. The pair moved back to Harmony to live by her parents and continue the translation during Emma's pregnancy. Martin Harris took over most of the scribe duties at that point. Tragically, Emma lost their first baby.
- After Oliver had moved in with Emma and Joseph and taken over as scribe, the three moved to Fayette to be with the Whitmer family, where Emma scribed some more for Joseph.
- Emma was baptized along with the saints in Colesville (including the Knight family), but intense persecution drove them away before she could be confirmed. Joseph was also receiving revelation that he shouldn't worry about material things and should focus on his ministry. In the face of her worries and concern, Joseph received a revelation in July 1830 that reminded her that she was blessed and an "elect lady". She was given greater perspective and asked to support her husband, in addition to being asked to create a hymnal **[Section 25]**.
- Emma accompanied Joseph as they moved between Harmony, Pennsylvania, and the Whitmer farm in Fayette, New York. They eventually moved to Ohio in early 1831 and lived on the Morely farm. Emma gave birth to twins, who died shortly after birth, but was able to immediately adopt twins who had lost their mother in childbirth that same day.
- By the fall of 1831, after Joseph returned from Missouri, Emma and Joseph moved into the Johnson home in Hiram, Ohio. While Joseph was being violently tarred and feathered one night, one of their twins was exposed to the freezing cold, and never recovered, passing away shortly thereafter.

Hyrum Smith

- Hyrum was Joseph's older brother!
- After Oliver Cowdery had joined Joseph to help in transcription, and after Hyrum's younger brother Samuel had become converted and baptized, Hyrum traveled from New York to Harmony, Pennsylvania. In May 1829, Hyrum asked Joseph for a revelation on his behalf, and Joseph received revelation about how Hyrum should gain knowledge to prepare for a future mission call **[Section 11]**.
- The following month, Hyrum was one of the Eight Witnesses to the Book of Mormon, along with his brother Samuel, and their father Joseph.
- After the Book of Mormon was published and the church was organized, Hyrum asked Joseph what his duties should be in the new church. In April 1830, along with 4 other brethren, Hyrum was given a revelation that he is under no condemnation. He was also specifically counseled that his heart and tongue are ready to preach and strengthen the church **[Section 23]**.
- Hyrum served as the leader of the "Colesville" branch of saints in New York, before Newel Knight took over as their leader.
- Once in Ohio in June of 1831, Hyrum was called to travel to Missouri along with Joseph, his companion John Murdock, and other brethren **[Section 52]**. Hyrum stayed in Missouri for a while and helped build up the church there.

Joseph Smith

(Since Joseph was involved in almost every Section of the Doctrine and Covenants, this entry on him also serves as a great overview for the entire church history surrounding Sections 1-70. I've kept it as brief as possible, while also making sure you can clearly see the big picture!)

- In the spring of 1820 and after pondering the scriptures, Joseph received a revelation and vision known as the First Vision, where God the Father and Jesus Christ appeared to him, promising him further knowledge later, forgiving him of his sins, and telling him not to join any church.
- Three years after the First Vision, the Angel Moroni came to visit Joseph. He told Joseph about golden plates hidden in a nearby hill, and repeated his message 3 more times **[Section 2].**
- Joseph went and found the golden plates and other relics buried in a nearby hill, but Moroni forbade him to touch them, and instead told him to return in a year. This happened every year until 1827, when Joseph was able to retrieve the plates.
- Joseph married Emma Hale when they eloped in 1827.
- After getting the plates, many people tried to steal the plates or harm Joseph, so Joseph and Emma moved from Palmyra, New York, to Harmony, Pennsylvania (near Emma's parents).
- Emma scribed for Joseph as he started his translation for a while, but soon Martin Harris came and took the position as scribe. To appease his hesitant wife, Martin asked for some pages of translated manuscript to show her. Unfortunately, Martin lost the manuscript pages, and remorsefully admitted to Joseph what had happened.
- Joseph received a revelation from the Lord about these lost pages, and subsequently lost his ability to translate for a few months in the summer of 1828 **[Section 3].**
- While still living in Harmony, Pennsylvania, Joseph was visited by his father, Joseph Sr. who asked for a revelation **[Section 4]**, and Martin Harris, who received a stern but comforting revelation **[Section 5].**
- Needing a new scribe, Joseph was pleased when Oliver Cowdery, a local school teacher, showed up in Harmony and offered to help. Joseph received a revelation for Oliver in April 1829 **[Section 6]**. The pair started translating immediately, and pondered about the fate of John the Beloved **[Section 7].**
- Oliver asked Joseph for the gift to translate the records, and was granted that permission via revelation, but then the permission was revoked **[Section 8-9]**. Soon after, Joseph received a revelation warning him that Satan was working with evil men for the missing manuscript pages, and that he shouldn't re-translate. **[Section 10].**
- Both Joseph's brother Hyrum and Joseph Knight, Sr (a family friend who had given Joseph assistance) asked for revelations in May 1829 **[Sections 11-12].**
- Joseph and Oliver, still in Harmony, pondered about baptism out in the woods. John the Baptist appeared and gave the two men the Aaronic priesthood in May of 1829 **[Section 13].**
- Due to growing oppression in Harmony, Joseph, Emma, and Oliver moved to the Peter Whitmer home in Fayette, New York to finish translation. David (Peter's son) was a friend of Oliver's. While at the Whitmer residence, Joseph received revelations for David **[Section 14]**, John **[Section 15]**, and Peter Jr. **[Section 16]** in June of 1829.
- Once the Book of Mormon translation was complete, Joseph received revelation that Oliver Cowdery, David Whitmer, and Martin Harris should be the Three Witnesses, and an angel showed them the gold plates in June of 1829 **[Section 17].**

- Joseph later showed the plates to eight additional witnesses, before returning the plates to an angel.
- He received revelations for Oliver and David about the organization of the church [Section 18], and for Martin, calling him to repentance during the summer of 1829 **[Section 19]**.
- It was time to officially organize a church! Joseph received many revelations in accordance with the church's organization in April of 1830 **[Sections 20-23]**. The church was organized at the Whitmer home in Fayette, with 6 official first members, but more than 40 women and men in attendance. Joseph and Oliver were both ordained, partook of the sacrament, and received the gift of the Holy Ghost.
- Around this time, Joseph started translating the Bible, with Oliver, Emma, and John Whitmer serving as scribes **[Section 35]**.
- During July 1830, Joseph received revelations for Oliver **[Section 24]**, Emma **[Section 25]**, and for himself, Oliver, and David **[Section 26]**. He later received revelation with more direction about the sacrament and putting on the armor of God **[Section 27]**.
- Joseph learned that Hiram Page (one of the Eight Witnesses) was using a seer stone to receive false revelations. Joseph prayed and received revelation for Oliver, telling Oliver to correct Hiram, and then telling him of his mission call to western Missouri in September of 1830 **[Section 27]**.
- A church conference was held in September 1830, and Joseph received a revelation prior to it **[Section 29]**. Peter Jr., Parley P. Pratt, and Ziba Peterson were called to accompany Oliver on his mission to the Native Americans **[Section 30, 32]**. Thomas B. Marsh was called to serve a mission as well, and promised blessings **[Section 31]**.
- The following couple of months, Joseph received additional revelations asking Ezra Thayre and Northrop Sweet to teach the gospel, and telling Orson Pratt that he is a Son of God **[Sections 33-34]**.
- When Sidney Rigdon and Edward Partridge arrived at Joseph's residence from Kirtland, Joseph received a revelation that Sidney should be his new scribe for the Bible translation **[Section 35]** and that Edward was called to a great work **[Section 36]**.
- Along with Sidney Rigdon, Joseph received the somewhat shocking revelation in December of 1830 that they should stop translating and that the church should move to Ohio [Section 37]. The people were promised at a church conference the following month that they would receive the fullness of the law once they had made the move **[Section 38]**.
- In January 1831, prior to the church's move to Ohio, Joseph received two revelations for James Covel, a Methodist minister, who almost converted, but then changed his mind **[Sections 39-40]**.
- The big move to Ohio happened! Joseph called Edward Partridge as the first Bishop of the church in Kirtland in February 1831 **[Section 41]**, and the new Law was given at a church conference with 12 elders **[Section 42]**. More revelation was received about how revelation for the entire church happens **[Section 43]**, and telling the elders to organize a church conference **[Section 44]**.
- In March of 1831, Joseph received a series of revelations while helping the saints become settled in Ohio and building up the new church. One revelation taught about the Second Coming and New Jerusalem **[Section 45]**; another revelation taught about spiritual gifts and allowing all to enter sacrament meetings **[Section 46]**; and another called John Whitmer to be the church historian **[Section 47]**. Joseph also received a revelation for the saints in Ohio to share their land with the new converts arriving from the eastern states **[Section 48]**.

- In May, Leman Copley approached Joseph, and Joseph received a revelation refuting many points of the Shaker religion **[Section 49]**. Joseph also received clarification about how to determine which spirits are of light and which one are of deception, a timely revelation due to the strange actions that had become commonplace during sermons in Ohio **[Section 50]**. Edward Partridge was given revelation about how to deal with the influx of new saints, and advising him to set up a bishop's storehouse **[Section 51]**.
- A church conference was held in June 1831 on Isaac Morley's farm in Kirtland. The Lord called Joseph and 27 other elders to go to Missouri in companionships and preach the gospel **[Section 52]**. In that same month, Joseph received some revelation for Sidney Gilbert **[Section 53]**, and for Newel Knight, commanding him to move all the Colesville saints in Thompson, Ohio to Missouri **[Section 54]**. William W. Phelps was told that he should be baptized, and move to Missouri to use his skills as a writer and printer **[Section 55]**, and Ezra Thayre was rebuked for selfishness **[Section 56]**.
- Joseph arrived in Jackson County, Missouri in July of 1831 for the very first time! He was likely a bit disappointed to see the land that was meant to be their Zion, but he received a revelation confirming that Independence was the location for Zion, and that the saints should start developing the land and settling down **[Section 57]**.
- In Missouri, Joseph received revelation for the church members who were arriving in the area about how to be anxiously engaged, and keep the Sabbath holy **[Sections 58-59]**.
- Eventually, in August of 1931, Joseph was given revelation that all the elders that had accompanied him on this mission were now ready to head back to Ohio **[Section 60]**. As they traveled back there were some disagreements and tensions that arose between the brethren, especially with Ezra Booth. Joseph received a revelation that the water was dangerous for them, but that they could travel anyway they wanted **[Section 61]**. As they continued to travel along the river, Joseph also was given revelation about how testimonies are recorded in heaven **[Section 62]**.
- Now back in Kirtland, Joseph received a revelation about only listening to official word on whether or not to stay in Ohio or travel to Missouri because the transition needed to happen slowly and orderly **[Section 63]**.
- Joseph was preparing to move to Hiram, Ohio in September of 1831 in order to continue working on his Bible translation, and received a revelation on forgiveness **[Section 64]**.
- In October of 1831, now back in Hiram, Ohio, Joseph received revelations about prayer and the gospel **[Section 65]**, and calling William McLellin to a mission **[Section 66]**.
- In response to very public criticisms from Ezra Booth, who was publishing accusatory articles about Joseph being secretive and having ulterior motives, Joseph proposed at a large meeting that all of his revelations up to that point should be published in a "Book of Commandments". **[Section 1]**. In November of 1831, the Book of Commandments was ratified and the elders were given a revelation addressing those who thought some of the revelations were written poorly **[Section 67]**.
- At this same conference, Joseph also received a revelation for four of the elders, reminding the saints that parents are to raise their children in righteousness **[Section 68]**. John and Whitmer were also tasked with taking the manuscript for the new Book of Commandments to Missouri in order to have it printed **[Section 69]**.
- Following this church conference, Joseph received a revelation when many of the elders were taught about being good stewards **[Section 70]**.

Joseph Smith, Sr.

- He was a very supportive father to Joseph, and was the first person that he told about many of the visions he experienced while growing up. He supported Joseph in keeping the plates hidden after he had obtained them. Joseph Jr. then moved with Emma to Harmony, Pennsylvania.
- After the fiasco with Martin Harris and the lost manuscript pages, Joseph Sr. was concerned about his son's well-being. He knew Joseph Jr. had lost the ability to translate for a while, and was concerned that he wasn't hearing from him as often. He went to visit Joseph Jr. in Harmony, Pennsylvania.
- While Joseph Sr. was in Harmony, discovering that his son was doing fine again, Joseph Jr. received a revelation for his father. **[Section 4]** This revelation in February 1829 spoke about Joseph Sr.'s desires and his qualification to do missionary work.
- Back at his home in Palmyra, New York, Joseph Sr. and his family hosted the local teacher, Oliver Cowdery, in their home. Oliver asked Joseph Sr. many questions about his son and his visions and plates. Joseph Sr. eventually opened up and that is what led Oliver to believe that he was called to assist Joseph in his work of translation.
- In June 1829, Joseph Sr. was able to be one of the Eight Witnesses of the Book of Mormon, along with his sons Hyrum and Samuel.
- After the Book of Mormon was published and the Church of Christ was formed, Joseph Sr. wanted to know what his duties in the new church would be. Joseph Jr. received a revelation for him and 4 other men who asked the same question **[Section 23]**. Joseph Sr. was told that he was under no condemnation and that he should strengthen the church in April 1830. Shortly thereafter, he was baptized into the church. Joseph Sr. remained a strong supporter of his son and the church.

Samuel H. Smith

- Samuel was the younger brother of the prophet Joseph!
- After their teacher, Oliver Cowdery, wished to go to Joseph and become his new scribe, Samuel is the one who accompanied Oliver from their family home in Palmyra, New York, to Joseph and Emma's home in Harmony, Pennsylvania.
- Later, Samuel went to visit his brother again, and Joseph preached the gospel to him. Samuel went into the woods alone, and came back with a firm witness that what his brother had taught him was true. He was baptized by Oliver Cowdery, and became one of the first traveling missionaries in the church.
- After the Book of Mormon was published and the church was organized, Samuel, along with 4 other brethren, asked Joseph what his duties should be in the new church in April 1830 **[Section 23]**. Samuel was given revelation that he was under no condemnation, and that he should strengthen the church.
- Samuel made the trip to Ohio with the rest of the church. In June 1831, at a conference of the church in Ohio, Samuel was called to travel to Missouri with Reynold Cahoon as his companion **[Section 52]**. A few months later in October, Samuel was called to serve a mission in the eastern states with William McLellin **[Section 66]**.

Northrop Sweet

- Northrop was a newly-baptized member of the church in Fayette, New York, who was given a revelation by Joseph in October 1830 that he should open his mouth and preach the gospel **[Section 33]**.
- Northrop departed from the church soon after this, and tried creating a new church which quickly failed.

Ezra Thayre

- Ezra had known Joseph and the Smith family previously, and was skeptical about the gospel until he heard Hyrum preach. He got baptized in Fayette, New York, and was given a revelation by Joseph in October 1830 that he should open his mouth and preach the gospel **[Section 33]**.
- After the move to Ohio, Ezra was called to travel to Missouri and preach the gospel **[Section 52]**, but that call was revoked pretty soon after, due to a rebuke for pride and selfishness **[Section 56]**.

Joseph Wakefield

- Joseph was baptized in Ohio, and told that the Lord was well pleased with him **[Section 50]**.
- In June of 1831, Joseph was called to travel to the eastern states with Solomon Humphrey, and to preach the gospel on their way there **[Section 52]**.

Joseph Wakefield

- Joseph was baptized in Ohio, and told that the Lord was well pleased with him **[Section 50]**.
- In June of 1831, Joseph was called to travel to the eastern states with Solomon Humphrey, and to preach the gospel on their way there **[Section 52]**.

Harvey Whitlock

- In Ohio, Harvey was called to travel to Missouri and preach the gospel on the way there with David Whitmer as his companion **[Section 52]**.

David Whitmer

- David became a good friend of Oliver Cowdery's while visiting Palmyra as Oliver was teaching. Both David and Oliver were curious about Joseph Smith, and Oliver wrote David many times to tell him about his desires to go help Joseph, and what the translation process was like after Oliver had arrived in Harmony.
- David lived in Fayette, New York with his parents, Peter and Mary, and many siblings. When Oliver wrote David, asking if his family could host Joseph, Emma, and Oliver as they finished the translation, David helped make that happen. He even experienced a miracle where his farm duties were partially completed, allowing him to help Joseph and Emma sooner than planned. David asked Joseph for a revelation once he was residing in their home in June 1829, and Joseph received one for him **[Section 14]**.
- David was moved with a righteous desire to be one of the Three Witnesses of the Book of Mormon, and was officially called to be one of them, seeing the plates in June 1829 **[Section 17]**. David was also given a revelation, along with Oliver, to repent because the worth of souls is great **[Section 18]**.
- Along with Joseph and Oliver, David was given a revelation about the law of common consent in July of 1830 **[Section 26]**. Two months later, following a church conference, David was given a revelation that he needed to be less focused on the things of the world, and fear God more **[Section 30]**.
- After the move to Ohio in June of 1831, David was called to travel to Missouri along with Joseph, his companion Harvey Whitlock, and other brethren **[Section 52]**.

John Whitmer

- John was David Whitmer's brother, also a son of Peter and Mary. Joseph stayed at John's father's residence in Fayette, New York to finish the translation of the Book of Mormon.
- John asked Joseph for a revelation while Joseph was at their home translating in June of 1829, and was given what is considered to be one of the most personal revelations, revealing that the Lord knew he had been asking for what would be the most worthwhile thing to do **[Section 15]**.
- John was one of the Eight Witnesses of the Book of Mormon, along with his brothers Christian, Jacob, and Peter Jr, and his brother-in-law Hiram Page. This witness occured at the Smith family farm in Manchester shortly after the Three Witnesses saw the plates in Fayette.
- Around this time, he became a scribe for Joseph as he translated the Bible **[Section 35]**.
- Following a church conference after the organization of the church, John was given revelation that he should preach the gospel and open his mouth **[Section 30]**.
- As the church was preparing to move to Ohio, Joseph sent John ahead of him with some copies of revelations to strengthen the new converts there. John was shocked at the variety of worship that he found.
- In March 1831, Joseph officially called John to be the church historian and recorder. John did not want the calling, but accepted it because he knew it came from the Lord **[Section 47]**.
- In November of that year, John and Oliver were called to accompany the manuscripts for the new Book of Commandments from Hiram, Ohio to Missouri for printing. John was also asked to travel from congregation to congregation, gathering a history of the church **[Section 69]**. He was also told to be a good steward with what he had been entrusted **[Section 70]**.

Peter Whitmer, Jr.

- Peter was David Whitmer's brother, and the son of Peter Sr. and Mary. Joseph stayed at his father's residence to finish the translation of the plates. While there, in June of 1829, Peter asked Joseph for a revelation, and was given a similar revelation to his brother, John **[Section 16]**.
- After the church was organized and following a church conference in September 1830, Peter was given a revelation that he should accompany Oliver on his mission to the Native American people in Missouri **[Section 30]**. Their mission took them to Kirtland first, where they converted many saints, and then took them to Western Missouri to preach to the Native American tribes.

Newel K. Whitney

- The Whitneys owned a store in Kirtland, and welcomed Joseph and Emma into their home after they first arrived in Ohio.
- In August and September of 1831, Newel was asked to stay in Kirtland in order to keep his store open, but to send whatever money he could to help Zion grow in Missouri **[Sections 63-64]**. Newel was also called to serve as the Bishop over the Saints in Ohio after Edward Partridge moved to Missouri.

Lyman Wight

- Lyman was a member of Sidney Rigdon's congregation, and resided at Isaac Morley's farm. He was converted and baptized, and later called to preach the gospel on a trip to Missouri **[Section 52]**. John Corrill was assigned as his companion, but Lyman was specifically warned that Satan wanted him.

Frederick G. Williams

- Frederick was one of the early converts in Kirtland, formerly a member of Sidney Rigdon's congregation. When Oliver, Parley, Peter, and Ziba came through preaching, he joined the 4 men for the rest of their journey to the Native Americans in the winter of 1830.
- After many in the church had been told to move to Missouri, Frederick was told in September of 1831 to not sell his farm in Kirtland, because the Lord wanted many saints to still stay there for a while **[Section 64]**.

PLACES

NEW YORK:

Manchester, NY

- This is where the Smith family lived.
- Joseph lived here when he experienced the First Vision in 1820, and when Angel Moroni appeared to tell him about the Book of Mormon in 1823.
- Joseph and Emma moved away from home after neighbors started becoming hostile, but the Smith family continued to reside here, giving Joseph a place to stay whenever he needed to come back home.
- Oliver Cowdery, a local school teacher, stayed here at the Smith home, which is where he learned about Joseph before offering to be Joseph's scribe.
- After the Book of Mormon was completely translated, the Eight Witnesses saw the gold plates in the woods by the Smith farm.
- Right after the official organization of the church in April 1830, Joseph came to Manchester a few times and received various revelations about baptism and mission calls.
- Eventually, after Joseph received revelation to move the church to Ohio, Joseph Smith Sr. and Lucy Mack Smith packed up their belongings and moved to Ohio in 1831.

Palmyra, NY

- Palmyra is the bigger town located right next to Manchester, where the Smith family farm was located.
- This is where E. B. Grandin's printing press printed the Book of Mormon in 1830.

Fayette, NY

- This is where the Whitmer family lived.
- Peter Whitmer Sr. owned a farm here, and many of his children lived with them. His son, David, became good friends with Oliver Cowdery, and Oliver stopped by their house on his way to go meet Joseph for the first time in Harmony. A few months later, Oliver asked the Whitmer family if he, Joseph, and Emma could move to their home while they finished the Book of Mormon translation, due to growing opposition in Harmony.
- The Book of Mormon translation was completed here at the Whitmer home in the summer of 1829, and Joseph received revelations for three of the Whitmer sons.
- It was here that Oliver, Martin, and David became the Three Witnesses to the Book of Mormon, and learned about the future organization of the church.
- On April 6, 1830, the "Church of Christ" was officially organized here in the Whitmer home. Joseph and Oliver ordained each other, and over 40 women and men were in attendance.
- This became the church headquarters for the remainder of 1830, with a church conference being held here in September. A few men received mission calls or other personal revelations during this conference. Many new prospective converts were sent to Fayette, and many were subsequently baptized or called on missions.
- In December 1830, Sidney Rigdon arrived from Ohio, curious to meet Joseph. These two men received the revelation that the saints should start preparing to move to Ohio. Although this announcement was met with some surprise, many saints started to make preparations, and left for Ohio during early 1831.

Colesville, New York

- The Knight family lived here.
- No official revelations in the Doctrine and Covenants were received here, but this is an important location to know because the Knight family, with Joseph Sr. and Polly at the head, played a huge role in the development of the church.
- Joseph Knight Sr. and his son Newel Knight had become good friends with Joseph, helping with Joseph and Emma's courtship and assisting Joseph later while he lived in Harmony. After the church was organized, many of the Colesville saints were baptized, and Colesville became like the second main branch of the church, after Fayette.
- Hyrum Smith was the leader of the saints in Colesville for a little while, but then Newel Knight took over as the leader. These saints were especially tight-knit, and always helped the poor and downtrodden among them.
- When it was time for the saints to move to Ohio, Newel and the Colesville saints traveled to Thompson, Ohio together.

PENNSYLVANIA:

Harmony, Pennsylvania

- Emma Hale Smith's family lived in Harmony.
- Following Joseph and Emma's successful retrieval of the gold plates, persecution in Manchester became so great that Emma and Joseph decided to move to be near her parents in Harmony.
- Emma scribed for Joseph here in Harmony until Martin Harris showed up and took over during her pregnancy. Emma lost her newborn baby, and Martin Harris lost the manuscript pages at around the same time, so Emma and Joseph mourned together over both losses here in late 1828.
- By early 1829, the translation was back on. Eventually, Oliver Cowdery showed up and offered to be Joseph's new scribe. They received many revelations together here, and the Aaronic priesthood was restored in the nearby woods.
- After persecution in Harmony started to grow, Joseph, Emma, and Oliver moved to Fayette to finish translating the Book of Mormon. They kept their home and farm in Harmony, returning from time to time throughout 1830 to tend to the farm, and take care of other business.
- By July 1830 though, it was revealed that Joseph should focus all his time and efforts on building up the church. The Lord gave Emma a special revelation in her time of uncertainty here in Harmony prior to their final departure.

OHIO:

Kirtland, Ohio

- Sidney Rigdon was a preacher in Kirtland, and had a strong congregation with devout followers. In late 1830, Oliver Cowdery, Parley P. Pratt, Peter Whitmer Jr., and Ziba Peterson were on their way from New York to western Missouri to preach the gospel, but Parley wanted to stop and talk to his former pastor Sidney Rigdon in Kirtland.
- The four-some ended up converting Sidney, his family, and most of his congregation, essentially doubling the size of the current church membership in November 1830.
- After the four brethren left to continue to Missouri, the new church members had some struggles figuring out spiritual gifts and organization. Sidney had left to go meet Joseph for the first time in New York, and these two men received the revelation that the church was to move to Ohio.
- Joseph and Emma officially moved to Ohio in the beginning of 1831. They resided in Kirtland at the Whitney home for a while. Edward Partridge was called as the Bishop, the Law was given, and Joseph clarified how revelation and gifts of the Spirit work.
- The saints in Kirtland had some growing pains while they welcomed in the members from New York, but the church continued to become more organized, with more callings being extended throughout March of 1831.
- After a big church conference in June of 1831, many men, including Joseph, were called to travel to Missouri for the first time to see Independence, where Zion would be built.
- After Joseph and many of the men returned to Kirtland in August of 1831, Joseph continued to preach, organize, and remind the saints that they were to stay in Kirtland until they were specifically called to move to Missouri. That call had only come to a few at this point, so the majority of the saints still resided in Kirtland by the end of 1831.

Hiram, Ohio

- Hiram was near Kirtland, Ohio, and this is where the John Johnson home was.
- The Johnson family welcomed Joseph and Emma into their home during the summer of 1831. Joseph made great progress on his translation of the Bible here.
- In November 1831, after Ezra Booth had started publishing terrible letters in the local newspaper about Joseph's secrecy, Joseph called a meeting of the church elders and proposed they publish all of his revelations so far in a Book of Commandments. This proposal was ratified, and the Lord gave them a revelation to use as the preface to the book (now Section 1).
- Joseph asked Oliver Cowdery and John Whitmer to accompany the Book of Commandments manuscript to Missouri so that William W. Phelps could publish the book, and the importance of that book was confirmed to many.

Thompson, Ohio

- When the saints from Colesville, New York, led by Newel Knight, followed the prophetic counsel to move to Ohio, they were all directed to settle in Thompson, Ohio on Leman Copley's land.
- Edward Partridge, the newly called bishop and Kirtland resident, needed some assistance in knowing how to help these saints from Colesville, and was thus given a revelation on how to enact the law of consecration and establish the first bishop's storehouse in May of 1831.
- Unfortunately, by June of 1831, Leman Copley had a change of heart and evicted the Colesville saints. Newel Knight sought direction on where they should go, and Joseph received an unexpected revelation that they should move to Missouri, becoming the first group of saints to settle in Independence.

MISSOURI:

Zion (Independence), Jackson County, Missouri

- The first saints to arrive in Independence were Oliver Cowdery, Parley P. Pratt, Peter Whitmer Jr., Ziba Peterson, and Frederick G. Williams, on their mission to the Native Americans in the winter of 1830.
- Joseph did not visit Missouri until July of 1831. There had been a lot of emotional buildup about this location where they would build up Zion, but there wasn't much special about Independence. Nonetheless, Joseph received confirming revelation that this is where Zion would be established, and certain saints were called to move to Missouri and set down roots.
- In August of 1831, Joseph and other elders returned back to Ohio after giving much counsel to the saints who were establishing the town. The group of members known as the "Colesville branch", who had briefly settled in Thompson, Ohio before being evicted, were the first group of saints to come to Missouri and played a huge role in its growth.

Along the Missouri River, Missouri

- Joseph and other companions of men were called to travel on a short mission for a church conference from Ohio to Missouri in the summer of 1831.
- After their short stay in Missouri, the group traveled back along the Missouri River. Mostly due to Ezra Booth, there were some arguments during this trip back. Joseph received a revelation that there was danger upon the water, but that all flesh was in God's hands.
- They also met another group of elders who were traveling from Ohio to Missouri, and Joseph received a revelation that testimonies are recorded in heaven.

DOCTRINE & COVENANTS

Part 1, Sections 1-70

little picture

Dive into each Section and apply the lessons to your life.

come follow me study

WITH CALI BLACK

SECTION 1

(Revelation to whole church about Doctrine and Covenants)

Through: Joseph Smith
To: the entire church
November 1831 in Hiram, Ohio

Even though most sections are chronological, the revelation for Section 1 was actually given after Section 66 at a special church conference. At this conference, the elders of the church agreed that all of these revelations (called the Book of Commandments at the time), should be compiled and published. The Lord gave this revelation as the "preface" to the Book of Commandments, which is why it is labeled as Section 1.

The Lord tells us to hearken to the word of the Lord and the prophets, and he declares the church to be true. We are asked to prepare the way of the Lord!

Apply this revelation to your life as you ponder:

- What does it mean to "hearken" to the prophets? What is an example you can think of where you have hearkened?

- Why does our Savior want us to search these prophecies contained in this book?

- Why do you think the Lord wanted these words specifically included as the first section in the Doctrine and Covenants?

SECTION 2

(Angel Moroni quoting Malachi to Joseph Smith about temple work)

Through: Angel Moroni
To: Joseph Smith
September 1823 in Manchester, New York

This section includes the words of the Angel Moroni to Joseph Smith. It is a small portion of Joseph Smith's history. Moroni quotes Malachi 4:5-6, with a few little changes in emphasis. This is the earliest revelation, chronologically, in the entire Doctrine and Covenants.

The Lord will reveal the keys through Elijah so the Earth is not wasted at his coming.

Apply this revelation to your life as you ponder:

- How has your heart been turned to your ancestors recently? If it hasn't, what can you do to feel this pull?

- Do you feel that the hearts of your ancestors have been turned toward you? How so?

- Why is temple work so important? How has it changed your life?

SECTION 3

(Revelation to Joseph Smith about the 116 lost pages)

Through: Joseph Smith
To: Joseph Smith
July 1828 in Harmony, Pennsylvania

This revelation was given to Joseph Smith after the loss of the 116 manuscript pages of the Book of Mormon.

The Lord declares that the designs of God will not be frustrated, and that we should not fear men more than we fear God.

Apply this revelation to your life as you ponder:

- How have you seen the Lord work miracles against impossible odds in your life?

- What natural consequence was Joseph Smith given after this transgression? How do you see natural consequences for sin in your life?

- Who do you fear more right now: the judgments of men, or the judgments of God? When have you felt both?

SECTION 4

(Revelation about being a missionary)

Through: Joseph Smith
To: Joseph Smith, Sr.
February 1829 in Harmony, Pennsylvania

Joseph Smith, Sr. visited his son in Pennsylvania to offer his support. While he was there, he asked his son for a revelation to know what the Lord wanted him to do.

In this great missionary revelation, the Lord talks about our desires and about the qualifications to do God's work.

Apply this revelation to your life as you ponder:

- How can we possibly stand blameless before God at the last day? What does this look like in your life?

- Do you desire to serve God and perform missionary work? How can you continue to grow that desire?

- What Christlike qualities is Joseph Smith, Sr. told are important?

SECTION 5

(Revelation for Martin Harris)

Through: Joseph Smith
To: Martin Harris
March 1829 in Harmony, Pennsylvania

After the debacle with the 116 pages, Martin Harris once again visited Joseph Smith. While he was there, Joseph received this revelation.

Martin is told to believe Joseph Smith's testimony, and that he can be one of the three witnesses of the Book of Mormon. The Lord talks about how believers receive a manifestation of the Spirit.

Apply this revelation to your life as you ponder:

- What blessings do we receive when we believe the words of Christ?

- What did the Lord ask Martin to do before receiving his witness? How can we follow this same pattern?

- What do we learn about the spiritual gifts that Joseph Smith has been given? Which spiritual gifts do you believe God wants you to focus on right now?

SECTION 6

(Revelation for Oliver Cowdery)

Through: Joseph Smith
To: Oliver Cowdery
April 1829 in Harmony, Pennsylvania

Oliver Cowdery, a schoolteacher, had heard of Joseph Smith from Joseph Smith, Sr. He had prayed and received a confirmation. He traveled to Pennsylvania to meet Joseph Smith.

The Lord reminds Oliver of the answer he had received. He teaches that when we inquire in faith, we are taught by the Spirit and encircled in the arms of his love.

Apply this revelation to your life as you ponder:

- What should we be "seeking" for in our lives?

- How do we learn the mysteries of God? Do you truly believe that you can learn mysteries if you ask God and exercise your spiritual gifts?

- What "further witness" does the Lord tell Oliver to think on? Have you received a witness like this before?

SECTION 7

(Translation of a record of John)

Through: Joseph Smith
To: Joseph Smith and Oliver Cowdery
April 1829 in Harmony, Pennsylvania

Joseph and Oliver were wondering what had happened to the apostle John. Joseph saw a parchment in a vision and translated it with the Urim and Thummim.

We learn that the apostle John will live on the earth until Christ's second coming.

Apply this revelation to your life as you ponder:

- What did Peter and John each desire? Reflect on your greatest desires right now.

- How can we find joy in doing different things than those around us?

- According to the section heading, why did Joseph Smith and Oliver Cowdery even receive this revelation? What can we learn from this?

SECTION 8

(Revelation for Oliver Cowdery about translating the Book of Mormon)

Through: Joseph Smith
To: Oliver Cowdery
April 1829 in Harmony, Pennsylvania

Oliver Cowdery wanted to translate the plates. Joseph asked the Lord and received this revelation.

The Lord grants Oliver's request and explains to him one of the ways that inspiration is received. He also talks about the importance of faith.

Apply this revelation to your life as you ponder:

- Which way to receive inspiration does the Lord teach about? Have you received personal revelation in this way before?

- What does the Lord teach about faith? What have you been able to accomplish with faith in your life?

- Why is it important to know that Oliver is the one who asked? What have you asked for from the Lord recently? What could you try asking for?

SECTION 9

(Revelation for Oliver Cowdery about translating the Book of Mormon)

Through: Joseph Smith
To: Oliver Cowdery
April 1829 in Harmony, Pennsylvania

Oliver Cowdery's attempt to translate the Book of Mormon didn't go very well and Joseph received this revelation.

This revelation revokes Oliver Cowdery's permission to translate. The Lord gives Oliver some direction and counsel about this, but also reminds Oliver that he is not condemned.

Apply this revelation to your life as you ponder:

- What do we learn about the Lord's characteristics from how he speaks to Oliver?

- What does the Lord teach us about asking him questions? What should we do before asking questions?

- Have you felt a burning bosom or a stupor of thought when asking questions in prayer? Reflect on the importance of those two responses.

- Have you ever been asked to have patience and to be content with what the Lord has given you right now?

SECTION 10

(Revelation to Joseph Smith about the 116 pages)

Through: Joseph Smith
To: Joseph Smith
April 1829 in Harmony, Pennsylvania

Joseph and Oliver were wondering whether they should retranslate the lost portion of the Book of Mormon.

This revelation reveals what wicked men are going to do with the 116 lost manuscript pages of the Book of Mormon. Review section 3 in order to get the first part of this story! This section shows the reality of Satan, but ultimately shows that those who pray will always come off conquerors.

Apply this revelation to your life as you ponder:

- What blessings come to us when we pray always? Have you seen this in your life?

- What do we learn about how Satan works? What patterns and strategies does he use? Can you see him using those today still?

- What did the Lord tell Nephi and Mormon to do to prepare for the error that Joseph Smith made?

SECTION 11

(Revelation to Hyrum Smith)

Through: Joseph Smith
To: Hyrum Smith
May 1829 in Harmony, Pennsylvania

Hyrum visited Joseph in Pennsylvania and Joseph received this revelation.

Hyrum is told to obtain God's word so that he can be effective in proclaiming the gospel when the time comes.

Apply this revelation to your life as you ponder:

- Where should we put our trust? How have you practiced this?

- What is Hyrum told to do while he waits for an official call to preach? How can we gather knowledge and doctrine while waiting for bigger assignments?

- What should we be seeking first? How can we make sure our priorities are in the correct order?

SECTION 12

(Revelation to Joseph Knight, Sr.)

Through: Joseph Smith
To: Joseph Knight, Sr.
May 1829 in Harmony, Pennsylvania

Joseph Knight, Sr. had employed Joseph Smith 4 years earlier. He was a believer and had been a friend of the Smith family and had given financial assistance to Joseph and Emma.

Joseph Knight, Sr. is told that when we work in God's kingdom and are humble, we will enjoy everlasting salvation.

Apply this revelation to your life as you ponder:

- What is Joseph Knight, Sr. asked to do by the Lord? How can we follow this, too?

- What qualities should those who assist in God's work have? How can we develop these?

- Why do you think Joseph Knight, Sr. asked for a revelation from God?

SECTION 13

(Words of John the Baptist to Joseph Smith and Oliver Cowdery)

Through: John the Baptist
To: Joseph Smith
May 1829 near Harmony, Pennsylvania

Joseph and Oliver had read about baptism while translating the Book of Mormon. They went to the woods to pray about it and were visited by John the Baptist.

These are the words of John the Baptist when he ordained Joseph Smith and Oliver Cowdery to the Aaronic Priesthood.

Apply this revelation to your life as you ponder:

- What specific keys does the Aaronic Priesthood include?

- How has the Aaronic Priesthood blessed your life? How can you feel more appreciation for this lesser Priesthood?

- How do you feel knowing that this Priesthood will never be taken from the earth again until Christ comes?

SECTION 14

(Revelation to David Whitmer about eternal life)

Through: Joseph Smith
To: David Whitmer
June 1829 in Fayette, New York

David Whitmer had learned about Joseph from Oliver Cowdery. The Whitmer family, headed by Peter and Mary, offered Joseph and Emma free room and board in Fayette, New York while they finished the translation of the Book of Mormon. (Sections 15 and 16 are revelations for David's brothers.)

The Lord teaches David that eternal life is the greatest gift of God, and we should stand as a witness of what we hear and see.

Apply this revelation to your life as you ponder:

- What is considered the greatest gift that God can give? What are you willing to do in order to receive this gift?

- How do you stand as a witness of the things that you hear and see?

- What is David called to do, and what blessings is he promised? What have you been called to do in your life, and what have you been promised?

SECTION 15

(Revelation to John Whitmer)

Through: Joseph Smith
To: John Whitmer
June 1829 in Fayette, New York

While Joseph and Emma stayed with the Whitmers, Joseph received this revelation for John Whitmer. (Sections 14 and 16 are revelations for John's brothers.)

The Lord teaches John that the thing of most worth to him will be to declare repentance to many people.

Apply this revelation to your life as you ponder:

- What is the thing that only John Whitmer and the Lord knew?

- What can you learn about John's character from his desire?

- What is the thing of most worth to John? Do you think this is also of the greatest worth in your life?

SECTION 16

(Revelation to Peter Whitmer, Jr.)

Through: Joseph Smith
To: Peter Whitmer, Jr.
June 1829 in Fayette, New York

While Joseph and Emma stayed with the Whitmers, Joseph received this revelation for Peter Whitmer, Jr. (Sections 14 and 15 are revelations for John's brothers.)

The Lord gives Peter a similar revelation as he did to John in Section 15, teaching him that the thing that is of most worth is to preach repentance to many people.

Apply this revelation to your life as you ponder:

- Why would the Lord give similar blessings and promises to two brothers?

- What are you currently desiring from the Lord?

- Why is preaching repentance such a worthwhile goal in life?

SECTION 17

(Revelation to the Three Witnesses of the Book of Mormon)

Through: Joseph Smith
To: Oliver Cowdery, David Whitmer and Martin Harris
June 1829 in Fayette, New York

The Book of Mormon says that there will be three witnesses. Oliver, David and Martin had felt inspired to be those witnesses.

This revelation called Oliver, David and Martin to be the Three Witnesses to the Book of Mormon. The Lord also gives his testimony of the Book of Mormon!

Apply this revelation to your life as you ponder:

- What specific items were they allowed to view? Review what you know about each of the items, their significance, use and history.

- What is the role of faith in seeing these items? Why do you think they needed to have faith in order to see them?

- What were they commanded to do after they had seen the plates and other items? Why do you think this part was important?

SECTION 18

(Revelation to Joseph Smith, Oliver Cowdery and David Whitmer)

Through: Joseph Smith
To: Joseph Smith, Oliver Cowdery and David Whitmer
June 1829 in Fayette, New York

Instructions are given to Joseph Smith, Oliver Cowdery and David Whitmer.

In the first part of this revelation, Oliver Cowdery is told that the church will be organized after the pattern in the Book of Mormon. Then, Oliver and David are told to repent because the worth of souls is great in the sight of God! They are also asked to start seeking out who will be the first twelve apostles.

Apply this revelation to your life as you ponder:

- How does knowing that the worth of souls is great in the sight of God affect your view of the world, yourself, and those you live around?

- Why do you think we feel great joy when we bring people unto the Savior? Have you felt that joy before?

- How are Oliver and David supposed to search out the Twelve? What kind of people are they looking for?

SECTION 19

(Revelation to Martin Harris)

Through: Joseph Smith
To: Martin Harris
Summer 1829 in Manchester, New York

Joseph Smith and Martin Harris are in negotiations with Egbert B. Grandin of Palmyra to print the Book of Mormon. No one among the early believers had the financial assets to fund the printing other than Martin Harris.

Martin is told to repent, and finance the printing of the Book of Mormon. This section is also notable because we get the firsthand account from our Savior on how difficult it was to perform his atoning sacrifice.

Apply this revelation to your life as you ponder:

- Why is it essential that we repent? What happens if we do? What happens if we do not?

- What emotions do you feel as you read about the Savior's account of his atoning sacrifice? How do your emotions while reading this push you to want to change?

- How do you feel peace in Christ?

(Revelation on the government and organization of the Church)

Through: Joseph Smith
To: The Church
April 1830 in Fayette, New York

As Joseph and Oliver and working towards the organization of the church, they have many questions.

This section is called the "Articles and Covenants" of the church. It lays out some of the basic doctrines and policies of the young church. It was essentially the general handbook of instructions at the time! It includes duties of various Priesthood offices, and verbiage for baptism and sacrament prayers.

Apply this revelation to your life as you ponder:

- Where do you see evidence that God is the same yesterday, today, and forever? How does that bring you peace?

- What important doctrines are included within this section?

- What are the duties of each office of the Priesthood? Whether or not you hold that office, how can you help fulfill those duties within the church?

SECTION 21

(Revelation to the Church on the day the Church was organized)

Through: Joseph Smith
To: The Church
April 1830 in Fayette, New York

This revelation was received during the organization of the church on April 6, 1830.

The members are called on to follow the prophet so that the gates of hell do not prevail.

Apply this revelation to your life as you ponder:

- What titles are Joseph called to? How do these titles differentiate from each other?

- How are we to treat the words of the prophets?

- What specific blessings are we promised if we listen to the prophets? Have you seen evidence of these in your life?

SECTION 22

(Revelation to the Church about baptism)

Through: Joseph Smith
To: The Church
April 1830 in Manchester, New York

Some believers wondered if they need to be re-baptized if they had already been baptized.

This revelation clarifies that even if someone has been baptized in another church, they must be re-baptized by proper authority into this church. Baptism by proper authority is the gate through which we must pass!

Apply this revelation to your life as you ponder:

- Which covenants did you make at baptism? How do those affect your life today?

- Why does proper authority matter when it comes to ordinances?

- How can we enter at the strait gate, and avoid dead works?

SECTION 23

(Revelation to various members)

Through: Joseph Smith
To: Oliver Cowdery, Hyrum Smith, Samuel H. Smith, Joseph Smith, Sr., and Joseph Knight, Sr.
April 1830 in Manchester, New York

Oliver Cowdery, Hyrum Smith, Samuel H. Smith, Joseph Smith, Sr., and Joseph Knight, Sr. all asked Joseph Smith what their duties should be. Joseph Smith inquired of the Lord, and these are all short responses with specific advice to each of the five men.

We learn that we should open our mouths and pray vocally, as well as in secret.

Apply this revelation to your life as you ponder:

- How do you avoid pride? What can you do to improve on this even more?

- How can you personally strengthen the church?

- What specific counsel do you think the Lord would give you? Have you tried asking recently?

SECTION 24

(Revelation to Joseph and Oliver)

Through: Joseph Smith
To: Joseph Smith and Oliver Cowdery
July 1830 in Harmony, Pennsylvania

This is a revelation given to Joseph Smith and Oliver Cowdery during a time of great persecution of the young church.

Joseph is told that he will have many afflictions in his life, but that the Lord will be with him through it all. Sections 25 and 26 were received at the same time.

Apply this revelation to your life as you ponder:

- Have you experienced moments where words were given to you in the very moment you needed them? How do you think you can cultivate more of those moments?

- What does the Lord ask us to do in our times of affliction? How have you tried to do this in your life?

- The Lord says about Oliver, "I am with him to the end." If you substitute your name in there, how do you feel? How does this make you want to act?

SECTION 25

(Revelation to Emma Smith)

Through: Joseph Smith
To: Emma Smith
July 1830 in Harmony, Pennsylvania

This is a revelation given to Emma Smith.

Emma is called to expound scriptures and exhort the church, to support her husband in his calling and to receive support from him. She is also called to make a selection of hymns. Sections 24 and 26 were received at the same time.

Apply this revelation to your life as you ponder:

- Why was Emma called an "elect lady"?

- How was Emma asked to support her husband, and how was he asked to support her?

- Does your soul delight in hymns? Which hymns have touched your heart?

SECTION 26

(Revelation about common consent)

Through: Joseph Smith
To: Joseph Smith, Oliver Cowdery and John Whitmer
July 1830 in Harmony, Pennsylvania

This is a revelation given to Joseph Smith, Oliver Cowdery and John Whitmer during a time of great persecution of the young church.

The law of common consent is given. Sections 24 and 25 were received at the same time.

Apply this revelation to your life as you ponder:

- How have you learned to study the scriptures, and how has it blessed your life?

- Do you have times where you are given directions for only the next step, and you have to take the step before you receive more information? How do you feel during these times?

- What does the "law of common consent" look like in your interactions with others in the church or your family? How can you cultivate this even more?

SECTION 27

(Revelation about the sacrament)

Through: Joseph Smith
To: The Church
August 1830 in Harmony, Pennsylvania

This is a message received by a heavenly messenger as Joseph was trying to procure wine for the sacrament.

Joseph is told that it doesn't matter what you eat or drink for the sacrament, as long as it is done while focused on God. In a future day, we will partake of the sacrament with ancient prophets and other righteous people.

Apply this revelation to your life as you ponder:

- Why do you think we currently use bread and water for our sacrament services?

- Which person would you be most excited to partake of the sacrament with someday?

- Which part of the armor of God are you best at "putting on"? Which is the hardest for you to "put on" right now?

SECTION 28

(Revelation about order in the church)

Through: Joseph Smith
To: Oliver Cowdery
September 1830 in Fayette, New York

Hiram Page, one of the eight witnesses of the Book of Mormon, was claiming to receive revelations for the whole church. Several members, including Oliver Cowdery, had been deceived.

The Lord teaches that only the prophet can receive revelations on behalf of everyone. Oliver Cowdery is called on a mission to the native tribes west of Missouri.

Apply this revelation to your life as you ponder:

- Do you know who you have the authority to receive revelation for, either in your callings or in your family? Do you know who you do not have the authority to receive revelation for?

- How do you think Oliver felt receiving this mission call?

- Do you think that Satan still deceives people today? How can you avoid being deceived?

SECTION 29

(Revelation about the coming of Christ)

Through: Joseph Smith
To: The Church
September 1830 in Fayette, New York

This revelation was given to Joseph Smith prior to a church conference, and he was with 6 other elders of the church.

The signs of Christ's coming are mentioned, and we are taught that all things are spiritual to the Lord. Christ also teaches us about the role of Satan and our agency.

Apply this revelation to your life as you ponder:

- Why are we asked to be glad? Do you feel good cheer from this gospel?

- What signs are given for Christ's Second Coming? How can we prepare for these coming events?

- What do we learn about the history and nature of Satan? How can learning about him help us to avoid his traps and learn his ways?

SECTION 30

(Revelation to the Whitmer brothers)

Through: Joseph Smith
To: David Whitmer, Peter Whitmer Jr., and John Whitmer
September 1830 in Fayette, New York

This section is actually a compilation of three separate revelations given through Joseph Smith to David Whitmer, Peter Whitmer, Jr., and John Whitmer right after their church conference.

The three brothers are commanded to be diligent, and Peter is called to join Oliver Cowdery on his mission to the native tribes west of Missouri.

Apply this revelation to your life as you ponder:

- What was David's stumbling block? When have you dealt with similar troubles, and how have you learned to rely on your Savior for all strength?

- How is Peter commanded to deal with his afflictions? What can you learn from this advice?

- How have you "opened your mouth" recently in declaring the gospel?

SECTION 31

(Revelation to Thomas B. Marsh)

Through: Joseph Smith
To: Thomas B. Marsh
September 1830 in Fayette, New York

This section is a revelation to Thomas B. Marsh, a new convert to the church.

Thomas is called to preach the gospel and promised that his family will be kept safe. He is asked to be patient in his afflictions and to not revile against those that revile.

Apply this revelation to your life as you ponder:

- What beautiful blessing does Thomas receive for his children? How would that make you feel?

- What kinds of success is Thomas promised? What can you do to build up the kingdom of God in your own way?

- What do you think it means to "revile not against those that revile"?

SECTION 32

(Revelation to Parley P. Pratt and Ziba Peterson)

Through: Joseph Smith
To: Parley P. Pratt and Ziba Peterson
October 1830 in Manchester, New York

This section calls Parley P. Pratt and Ziba Peterson on a mission.

Parley P. Pratt and Ziba Peterson are called to join Oliver Cowdery and Peter Whitmer on their mission to the native tribes. This mission will eventually take them through Kirtland, Ohio and Independence, Missouri – two places that are super important in the future of the church!

Apply this revelation to your life as you ponder:

- How do you maintain a meek and lowly heart?

- Parley and Ziba were promised that nothing would prevail against them. When we are righteous, we are promised that, too. When have you felt the hand of God lifting you up in a situation where you could have felt defeated?

- What blessings have you seen in your life as you have "prayed always"?

SECTION 33

(Revelation to Ezra Thayre and Northrop Sweet)

Through: Joseph Smith
To: Ezra Thayre and Northrop Sweet.
October 1830 in Fayette, New York

This revelation was given to newly-baptized members Ezra Thayre and Northrop Sweet.

Ezra Thayre and Northrop Sweet are called to open their mouths and invite people to repentance.

Apply this revelation to your life as you ponder:

- When did Nephi (in the Book of Mormon) open his mouth? How can he be a good example to us (And Ezra and Northrop) in speaking out for good?

- What is the foundational "rock" in your life?

- How do the Spirit and the scriptures work together in your life?

SECTION 34

(Revelation to Orson Pratt)

Through: Joseph Smith
To: Orson Pratt
November 1830 in Fayette, New York

This revelation was given to Orson Pratt, through Joseph Smith. Orson was 19 years old and a new convert after listening to his older brother, Parley, preach.

Orson Pratt is called a son of God and asked to cry repentance to prepare for the Lord's Second Coming.

Apply this revelation to your life as you ponder:

- What titles does the Savior use in these words? What do these titles mean to you?

- How does knowing that you are a son or daughter of God change you each day?

- How can you have sure faith, even when the world deals with wickedness and destruction?

SECTION 35

(Revelation to Joseph Smith and Sidney Rigdon)

Through: Joseph Smith
To: Joseph Smith and Sidney Rigdon
December 1830 in Fayette, New York

This revelation was given to Joseph Smith and the newly-baptized Sidney Rigdon, who had just traveled to New York from Ohio along with Edward Partridge.

Joseph Smith needed a new scribe for his translation of the Bible, and Sidney is called to take on that new position. He is reminded that God is still a God of miracles and that the prophet holds the keys to mysteries. This is a companion section to Section 36!

Apply this revelation to your life as you ponder:

- What "greater things" have you already experienced in your life? What "greater things" might still be available for you?

- What miracles have you seen? How do they grow your belief in God?

- How have you felt when being extended various callings in your life, especially if you felt inadequate for them?

SECTION 36

(Revelation to Edward Partridge)

Through: Joseph Smith
To: Edward Partridge
December 1830 in Fayette, New York

This revelation was given to Edward Partridge, who had traveled from Ohio to New York along with Sidney Rigdon.

The Lord tells Edward that he will give him the Spirit through the hands of Sidney. He is taught the importance of crying repentance. This is a companion section to Section 35!

Apply this revelation to your life as you ponder:

- When has the Holy Spirit acted as a comforter to you?

- How can you "embrace" the callings and commandments that you have been given?

- What does it look like in your life to cry repentance?

SECTION 37

(Revelation to Joseph Smith and Sidney Rigdon calling the church to move to Ohio)

Through: Joseph Smith
To: Joseph Smith, Sidney Rigdon and the Church
December 1830 in Fayette, New York

This revelation contains the first commandment in the dispensation for the saints to gather.

The church is called to leave New York and Pennsylvania, and go to Ohio.

Apply this revelation to your life as you ponder:

- How has the Lord protected you from the enemy in your life?

- What does it mean to pray "in faith"? Do you do this in your prayers?

- What is the role of agency in everything that the Lord asks us to do?

SECTION 38

(Revelation to the Church at a conference)

Through: Joseph Smith
To: The Church
January 1831 in Fayette, New York

This revelation was given through Joseph Smith at a church conference.

The Lord tells the members that they are to be one, and to esteem their brothers as themselves. The poor should be taken care of, and the Saints are told that they will receive the law once they make the move to Ohio.

Apply this revelation to your life as you ponder:

- What does it mean to you to "esteem your brother as thyself"? How can you try to do this within the next week?

- How can you build unity within your family, your ward/branch, and your local community?

- How does the church care for the poor and the needy? How can you help in this important work?

SECTION 39

(Revelation to James Covel)

Through: Joseph Smith
To: James Covel
January 1831 in Fayette, New York

A Methodist minister named James Covel had covenanted to obey any commands that the Lord gave him through Joseph Smith.

The Lord calls James Covel to be baptized and preach the gospel. This is a companion section to Section 40!

Apply this revelation to your life as you ponder:

- How do we become sons (or daughters) of Christ?

- What did the Lord see in James' heart? What might he see in yours right now?

- It seemed like James had originally hoped to serve a mission in the eastern states/countries, but the Lord had something greater in mind for him. Have you experienced anything like this before?

SECTION 40

(Revelation to James Covel)

Through: Joseph Smith
To: James Covel
January 1831 in Fayette, New York

James Covel, the Methodist minister, rejected the commandment he had received in Section 39.

James Covel, the Methodist minister, rejected the commandment he had received in Section 39 because he was afraid of persecution and the cares of the world. Joseph Smith and Sidney Rigdon received this revelation. This is a companion section to Section 39!

Apply this revelation to your life as you ponder:

- What things have you covenanted with the Lord to do?

- When was the most recent time that Satan tempted you? How have you learned to overcome temptations?

- How do you learn to not care about the reactions of people "in the world" as you follow Christ? What more can you do in order to change your mindset?

SECTION 41

(Revelation to the Church at Kirtland, Ohio)

Through: Joseph Smith
To: The Church
February 1831 in Kirtland, Ohio

This is the first section of revelation received in Kirtland, Ohio! It was given through Joseph Smith to the entire church.

The members are called to become disciples, and asked to pray for the law to be given to them. Joseph is told to build a house, while Sidney Rigdon can live anywhere he wants. Edward Partridge is called as the first Bishop in the church. This section leads up to the "Law" being given in Section 42!

Apply this revelation to your life as you ponder:

- Why do you think the Lord requires work before giving any kind of revelation or commandment?

- How do we become disciples to our Savior?

- What quality does the Lord recognize in Edward's heart? How can you develop a more pure heart?

SECTION 42

(Revelation to the Church at Kirtland, Ohio)

Through: Joseph Smith
To: The Church
February 1831 in Kirtland, Ohio

This section is the revelation known as "The Law" that was promised originally in Section 38. Verses 1-72 are the law, and the revelation was received in front of 12 elders in the church.

In verses 1-72, elders are called on missions, rules for consecration are explained, and various other commandments are given. Verses 73-93 are about "embracing the Law of the church" and include some details on how to deal with those who break commandments.

Apply this revelation to your life as you ponder:

- Which "law" stands out to you as one that you need to personally focus on right now in your life?

- How is consecration a blessing in the church today?

- What are church members promised when they ask the Lord? How have you seen examples of this?

SECTION 43

(Revelation to the Church at Kirtland, Ohio)

Through: Joseph Smith
To: The Church
February 1831 in Kirtland, Ohio

Some members of the young church were saying that they could receive revelation for the whole church. This section was given through Joseph Smith to the entire church, and the elders of the church who had been called on missions.

The Lord clarifies that only the one who is appointed can receive revelations for all of the members. The elders of the church are told to repent more, call upon heaven, and preach repentance.

Apply this revelation to your life as you ponder:

- Who do you currently have authority to receive revelation for?

- Why were the church members asked to assemble together? What value do you see in assembling together with church members?

- How does knowing what will come in the Millennium change your actions now?

SECTION 44

(Revelation to the Joseph Smith and Sidney Rigdon)

Through: Joseph Smith
To: Joseph Smith and Sidney Rigdon
February 1831 in Kirtland, Ohio

A revelation to Joseph Smith and Sidney Rigdon.

Joseph and Sidney receive a revelation that the church should have a conference. When they assemble, the Lord will pour out his Spirit. The church is also told to provide for the poor and the needy.

Apply this revelation to your life as you ponder:

- Have you ever experienced the Lord's Spirit being poured out on you in a group setting? What do you remember from it?

- Why are church conferences so important?

- Why do you think the Lord needed to include the importance of taking care of the needy in so many revelations?

SECTION 45

(Revelation to the Church)

Through: Joseph Smith
To: The Church
March 1831 in Kirtland, Ohio

A revelation to the Church.

Joseph received this glorious revelation while rumors and false reports about the church were circling. The revelation teaches that Christ is our advocate with the Father, and that he is a light to the world. Signs of the Second Coming are taught. The Saints are asked to build New Jerusalem.

Apply this revelation to your life as you ponder:

- What roles and descriptions of the Savior can you find in this Section? Which stands out to you as the most prominent right now?

- How can we avoid being deceived at the final day, just as in the parable of the ten virgins?

- What qualities will the New Jerusalem have? How can you build those qualities in your home today?

SECTION 46

(Revelation to the Church)

Through: Joseph Smith
To: The Church
March 1831 in Kirtland, Ohio

A revelation to the Church.

Joseph was given this revelation because a habit of only letting church members and serious investigators into church services had started to occur. The Lord teaches that everyone should be allowed into sacrament meetings. He also teaches about spiritual gifts, and lists some of them.

Apply this revelation to your life as you ponder:

- How can you help visitors feel more welcome during a church meeting?

- How do we avoid being deceived? Have you felt like you've been deceived before?

- Why are we given spiritual gifts? Which gifts do you have, and which ones would you like to develop? (Keep in mind that only a few gifts are actually listed in this Section.)

SECTION 47

(Revelation to John Whitmer)

Through: Joseph Smith
To: John Whitmer
March 1831 in Kirtland, Ohio

A revelation to John Whitmer, who was serving as a clerk to Joseph Smith.

John Whitmer, after serving as a clerk to Joseph Smith for a time, was called to serve as church historian (replacing Oliver Cowdery). John hesitated at first, but ultimately accepted and served in his office.

Apply this revelation to your life as you ponder:

- Have you ever been asked to do something you don't want to do? How did you respond?

- How do you balance doing things that bring your joy, and things that stretch your abilities?

- Why do we keep a church history? Why is knowing our history important?

SECTION 48

(Revelation to the Church)

Through: Joseph Smith
To: The Church
March 1831 in Kirtland, Ohio

A revelation to the Church.

Joseph Smith receives a revelation that the Saints in Kirtland should share their land with new converts as they arrive, and save money while preparing to build a city.

Apply this revelation to your life as you ponder:

- How do we help welcome new converts into our wards and neighborhoods?

- What is the spiritual importance for saving money? How can you do better at saving?

- Why do you think the church places an importance on being organized and listening to our local leaders, in addition to churchwide leaders?

SECTION 49

(Revelation to Sidney Rigdon, Parley P. Pratt and Leman Copley about the Shakers)

Through: Joseph Smith
To: Signey Rigson, Parley P. Pratt and Leman Copley
May 1831 in Kirtland, Ohio

Leman Copley was a member of the church, but had previously belonged to the Shakers and still believed some of their principles.

This revelation refutes some of the Shaker beliefs, including clarifying that the Second Coming is still in the future and that marriage is ordained of God.

Apply this revelation to your life as you ponder:

- Why do you think the exact time that the Lord is returning is kept as a surprise? How are you preparing for the Second Coming?

- Why is marriage ordained of God? How have righteous marriages been a blessing in your life?

- How do you remain steadfast, even when the world is in turmoil?

SECTION 50

(Revelation to the Church)

Through: Joseph Smith
To: The Church
May 1831 in Kirtland, Ohio

Joseph Smith received this revelation in response to some confusion about receiving visions from various spirits.

This revelation teaches that there are false spirits and righteous spirits, and the true spirit brings light. Members are asked to preach and listen with the spirit in order to know that it is a righteous spirit. Joseph Wakefield and Parley P. Pratt are called to help preach the gospel, John Corrill is called to labor in the vineyard, and Edward Partridge is called to repent.

Apply this revelation to your life as you ponder:

- How can you avoid being deceived, or avoid being a hypocrite?

- Have you reasoned with God before? Why does He use both feelings and logical reasoning in order to teach us truth?

- When you teach in church or in your family, how do you make sure you are teaching with the spirit of light?

SECTION 51

(Revelation to Edward Partridge)

Through: Joseph Smith
To: Edward Partridge
May 1831 in Thompson, Ohio

Members from the eastern United States had been arriving in Kirtland.

This revelation teaches Bishop Edward Partridge about how to provide for all the new saints arriving in Ohio. The Lord also teaches more about the law of consecration, and established the first bishop's storehouse.

Apply this revelation to your life as you ponder:

- How can we be wise stewards with what the Lord has given us?

- How do you keep the law of consecration as much as possible in your family right now?

- Have you been to a bishop's storehouse before? What do you know about these locations? (Do a quick online search if not!)

SECTION 52

(Revelation to the Elders of the Church)

Through: Joseph Smith
To: The Elders of the Church
June 1831 in Kirtland, Ohio

A revelation given to the Elders of the Church at the end of a church conference.

The Lord tells them that the next conference will be held in Missouri, which will be Joseph Smith's first trip there! Various other pairs are called to go to Missouri and preach along the way.

Apply this revelation to your life as you ponder:

- What does "contrite" mean? How can we keep our spirits contrite?

- What prerequisites does the Lord ask for when it comes to revealing truth and knowledge to us? How can we seek after this?

- What has the Comforter taught you recently? How can you seek to feel the Comforter in your life more often?

SECTION 53

(Revelation to Algernon Sidney Gilbert)

Through: Joseph Smith
To: Algernon Sidney Gilbert
June 1831 in Kirtland, Ohio

This revelation was given t0 Algernon Sidney Gilbert.

Algernon Sidney Gilbert is called to forsake the world and endure to the end!

Apply this revelation to your life as you ponder:

- What does it look like to "forsake the world"? How can you do that even more?

- What have you been ordained or set apart to do, specifically?

- What is one way that you have "endured" this week?

SECTION 54

(Revelation to Newel Knight and the Thompson Saints)

Through: Joseph Smith
To: Newel Knight
June 1831 in Kirtland, Ohio

Members of the church from Colesville, New York had moved to Kirtland and settled in the nearby town of Thompson. They were having trouble living the law of consecration, so Newel Knight, a leader, asked for some direction from Joseph Smith.

This revelation tells them to travel to Missouri and start making a living there and it tells them to be patient in tribulation.

Apply this revelation to your life as you ponder:

- What covenants have you made with your Heavenly Father? How are you working to keep them?

- Why are we asked to be patient when we are experiencing hard times?

- Why do you think the Lord wants us to remember often that he was crucified for us?

(Revelation to William W. Phelps)

Through: Joseph Smith
To: William W. Phelps
June 1831 in Kirtland, Ohio

This revelation was given to William W. Phelps.

This revelation was given to William W. Phelps. He was called to be baptized, and to write and print books for the church. He is also asked to go to Missouri.

Apply this revelation to your life as you ponder:

- It can be a lifelong process to continue "receiving the Holy Ghost" in our lives. How can you work on this every day?

- What does the Lord say is pleasing to him? How can we assist in teaching young kids the gospel?

- How do you use your specific talents, or even your profession, to build up the kingdom of God?

SECTION 56

(Revelation with instructions for various members)

Through: Joseph Smith
To: Ezra Thayre, Newel Knight and others
June 1831 in Kirtland, Ohio

This revelation contains instructions for several members.

This revelation holds a rebuke for Ezra Thayre. It also calls Newel Knight to travel with the Colesville Branch to settle in Missouri.

Apply this revelation to your life as you ponder:

- What examples can you think of when the Lord has commanded something, and then revoked it due to unrighteousness? Either personally, or in the church/scriptures?

- How are you working to root out any pride and selfishness in your life?

- What is the difference between the poor who are blessed, and the poor who are told "wo unto you"?

SECTION 57

(Revelation to the elders of the church in Jackson County, Missouri)

Through: Joseph Smith
To: The elders of the church
July 1831 in Zion, Jackson County, Missouri

Welcome to Jackson County, Missouri! Joseph Smith is here for the first time.

This revelation declares Independence, Missouri as the center place to the City of Zion. Sidney Gilbert is asked to start up a store, William W. Phelps is asked to be a printer, and Oliver Cowdery is asked to assist in editing materials for publication.

Apply this revelation to your life as you ponder:

- How does knowing that the Lord works in wisdom help our faith grow?

- Why is it helpful to have people with different strengths and gifts in one place? How are other people's strengths helpful to you, and vice versa?

- When we are given new counsel by the prophet, how do you work to "speedily" implement it in your life?

SECTION 58

(Revelation to the elders of the church in Jackson County, Missouri)

Through: Joseph Smith
To: The elders of the church
August 1831 in Zion, Jackson County, Missouri

This revelation was given for the saints who were starting to arrive in Missouri.

The saints were called to endure much, and taught that blessings come after tribulation. They are also counselled to do good works of their own free will, and repent of their sins by confessing and forsaking. Some people are called specifically to repent.

Apply this revelation to your life as you ponder:

- How do you feel knowing that blessings can come long after a trial? What have been your experiences with that?

- What good things have you chosen to do of your own free will recently? How can you do this even more?

- Why does the Lord often reveal things slowly, from time to time? How have you seen this in your life?

SECTION 59

(Revelation to the Church in Jackson County, Missouri)

Through: Joseph Smith
To: The Church
August 1831 in Zion, Jackson County, Missouri

This revelation was given for the saints who were starting to arrive in Missouri.

The Lord teaches how to keep the Sabbath Day holy, and how to fast and pray. They were also instructed that the things that come from the earth are for the benefit and use of man.

Apply this revelation to your life as you ponder:

- How have you made an effort to keep the Sabbath Day holy? Have you felt it keeping you spotless from the world?

- What are your current emotions related to fasting? How can it become more joyful?

- Does nature "please your eye" and "gladden your heart"? What is your favorite place to be in nature?

SECTION 60

(Revelation to the elders who had travelled to Missouri)

Through: Joseph Smith
To: The elders
August 1831 in Independence, Missouri

This revelation was given for those elders who had traveled to Missouri and were now going back to Ohio.

The elders are asked to open their mouths and share their talents, while not idling away their time.

Apply this revelation to your life as you ponder:

- How can you "open your mouth" more about the Savior?

- When are you tempted to be idle? How can you work to avoid idleness, and what can you replace it with instead?

- What kinds of excuses might make it easy for you (or others) to hide talents instead of sharing them?

SECTION 61

(Revelation to Joseph Smith)

Through: Joseph Smith
To: Joseph Smith and the Elders returning to Ohio
August 1831 in Independence, Missouri

This revelation was given as Joseph Smith and others were returning to Ohio.

This revelation teaches that there is danger declared upon the waters, but ultimately, all flesh is in God's hand.

Apply this revelation to your life as you ponder:

- Why do you think the Lord asks missionaries to serve in pairs?

- How can you make sure you aren't passing by people who truly need your help, even though you may be headed to do something else good?

- How does it help you to know that God has not forsaken you?

SECTION 62

(Revelation to Joseph Smith)

Through: Joseph Smith
To: Joseph Smith and the Elders returning to Ohio
August 1831 in Independence, Missouri

This is another revelation given while everyone was traveling back from Missouri to Ohio.

The traveling party met a group who were traveling to Missouri, and were told that the testimonies they bore were recorded in heaven. Bearing their testimonies can also result in a forgiveness of sins.

Apply this revelation to your life as you ponder:

- How has the Lord "succored" or supported you in your temptations?

- When was the last time that you bore your testimony (verbally or mentally)? When can you plan on doing this again in the future?

- When have you felt that the Lord left decisions up to your own judgment and directions of the Spirit?

SECTION 63

(Revelation to the Church)

Through: Joseph Smith
To: The Church
August 1831 in Kirtland, Ohio

Joseph is back in Ohio and received this revelation.

This revelation teaches that faith does not come from seeing signs, and that all of the saints should strive to build up Zion.

Apply this revelation to your life as you ponder:

- What signs have you seen in your life to know that God exists and loves you?

- Why do you think God only gives signs to those who have faith first? Have you seen examples of this?

- How has giving money to people in need been a blessing in your life?

SECTION 64

(Revelation to the Church)

Through: Joseph Smith
To: The Elders of the Church
September 1831 in Kirtland, Ohio

A revelation given to the elders of the Church.

In this revelation, the saints commanded to forgive one another and let God be the ultimate judge. Those who paid tithing would be saved, and Zion will flourish. They are also asked to not be weary in well-doing.

Apply this revelation to your life as you ponder:

- Who are we required to forgive? When has this been difficult for you, and when has this been easy?

- What do we need to do in order to repent and be forgiven by God?

- Have you felt weary in well-doing before? How have you overcome that?

SECTION 65

(Revelation to the Church)

Through: Joseph Smith
To: The Church
October 1831 in Hiram, Ohio

A revelation given to the Church.

Joseph received this revelation affirming that the gospel will eventually fill the entire earth. We are asked to pray that God's kingdom will go forth.

Apply this revelation to your life as you ponder:

- How have you seen the gospel grow to fill the earth even more during your lifetime?

- How can you prepare for the Savior's return?

- What things are we counselled to pray for? Have you tried praying for these things before?

SECTION 66

(Revelation answering William E. McLellin's questions)

Through: Joseph Smith
To: William E. McLellin
October 1831 in Hiram, Ohio

A man named William E. McLellin privately asked the Lord to answer five specific questions. He then went to Joseph and asked for a revelation, without telling him the questions.

This section answers William E. McLellin's questions, which include William's cleanliness, purpose, and a mission call.

Apply this revelation to your life as you ponder:

- What specific questions have you asked the Lord recently? Why do you think we've been asked to ask specific questions in prayer?

- What have been your experiences with blessings of healing?

- How has being patient been a blessing in your life?

SECTION 67

(Revelation to the assembled elders)

Through: Joseph Smith
To: The assembled elders of the Church
November 1831 in Hiram, Ohio

This revelation was given during a special conference where it was decided to publish the revelations as the Book of Commandments. It was given right after the revelation for Section 1. The book was to be published in Missouri, but some of the elders thought that the revelations could have been written better.

The Lord challenges any of the elders to create their own revelations, which they failed at. They will only see the Lord if they have true faith.

Apply this revelation to your life as you ponder:

- How are you working to root out fears that you may have in your heart?

- How do you show grace to other people when you discover their imperfections?

- How do you work on staying focused and forward-facing, instead of letting your mind turn back?

SECTION 68

(Revelation to the assembled elders)

Through: Joseph Smith
To: Orson Hyde, Luke S. Johnson, Lyman E. Johnson and William E. McLellin
November 1831 in Hiram, Ohio

This revelation was given specifically to Orson Hyde, Luke S. Johnson, Lyman E. Johnson, and William E. McLellin.

When those who are called to teach do so by the Holy Ghost, it is the word of the Lord. Parents are commanded to teach their children and have them baptized at age eight.

Apply this revelation to your life as you ponder:

- Have you ever felt the Spirit guiding words that you speak or write? How can you righteously seek after more opportunities like that?

- What are you doing to directly teach your children, or children that you interact with, the gospel? How can you improve in these efforts?

- How can you avoid teaching children to be idle?

SECTION 69

(Revelation to Oliver Cowdery and John Whitmer)

Through: Joseph Smith
To: Oliver Cowdery and John Whitmer
November 1831 in Hiram, Ohio

A revelation to Oliver Cowdery and John Whitmer about the publication of the revelations.

Oliver Cowdery and John Whitmer are called to take the manuscript for the Book of Commandments, as well as other money and resources, to Missouri for publication. John is also asked to write a history of the church. (Section 133 was given at this time, and was considered an "appendix" to the book, until it was officially assigned a section number.)

Apply this revelation to your life as you ponder:

- Why is more than one person tasked with handling important resources, including money? Why would the Lord find this pattern important?

- Why do we keep track of our history? What value have you found in studying your own personal and family history?

- What are your habits right now for recording your own history? How can you improve these habits?

SECTION 70

(Revelation to Joseph Smith, Martin Harris, Oliver Cowdery, John Whitmer, Sidney Rigdon, and William W. Phelps)

Through: Joseph Smith
To: Joseph Smith, Martin Harris, Oliver Cowdery, John Whitmer, Sidney Rigdon, and William W. Phelps
November 1831 in Hiram, Ohio

This revelation was given to Joseph, Martin Harris, Oliver Cowdery, John Whitmer, Sidney Rigdon, and William W. Phelps following the church conference where they ratified the importance of the revelations in the Book of Commandments.

They are counseled about the importance of stewardship and how to be righteous stewards.

Apply this revelation to your life as you ponder:

- What or who do you currently have stewardship over right now? (In callings, in your family...) How will you account to the Lord for what you are doing with that stewardship?

- How do you feel knowing that everyone in the church, including church leaders, have the same command to pay tithing?

- How have you learned to not give "begrudgingly" whenever you donate your time or money?

Thank you for supporting Come Follow Me Study!

For more resources, daily posts, or to sign up for my emails, head to comefollowmestudy.com or find me on Instagram at @comefollowmestudy.

If this is a digital download, you may print enough copies for members of your household who reside at the same address. Please do not share this digital file, or any portions thereof, with others. To purchase additional copies or to ask for special permissions, contact Cali Black at comefollowmestudy.com.

Made in United States
Troutdale, OR
12/02/2024